Para
Javier,
¡Adelante! —

¡Viva la Raza!
1-31-01

Small-Town Browny

Cosecha de la Vida

Other books with artwork by Simón Silva:

La Mariposa
By Francisco Jiménez

Gathering the Sun
By Alma Flor Ada

El Campo
By Juan Delgado

Small-Town Browny

Cosecha de la Vida

Simón Silva

Arte Cachanilla

Published by Arte Cachanilla

3197 North "G" Street, San Bernardino, CA 92405

Copyright © 1998 Simón Silva
All rights reserved under International and Pan American Copyright Conventions.
Published in the United States by Arte Cachanilla, San Bernardino, California.

Visit Simón Silva's Web site at
http://silvasimón.com

ISBN   0 - 9666241 - 0 - 6

Printed in the United States of America
First Edition
10 9 8 7 6 5 4 3 2 1

Book design and art by Simón Silva

Dedicated to

Mario Mange
May you rest in Peace.

For all past, present, and future *Campesinos*.

For anyone that has ever felt alone, frustrated,
unimportant, insignificant, or invisible.

*Y para toda mi Raza. ¡Especialmente para
aquellos que les gusta el pedo!*

¡Adelante!

Contents

Preface

This book is a response to all the great literature that I've
had the pleasure to read. It has been through literature that I
have been able to find my faults and strengths both as a human
being and as an artist. It is my hope that these stories, which
come from my adolescence, will evoke conversations about
experiences that remain to be discussed and examined. I hope
these stories will speak and bring respect to all of you who
might consider yourselves invisible. You are my inspiration,
and you can rest assured that you will live forever in my
thoughts.

Simón Silva

Cockfight Vacations

*G*rowing up I always dreaded going back to school
after any vacation. Everyone would share their bullshit
vacation stories, complete with show-and-tell
memorabilia. Being asked to share my experiences made
my stomach nauseous and my imagination squirm as I
contemplated the story I was about to fabricate. For
instance, an uneventful season of working in the carrot
fields would be magically replaced with a visit to my
scientific *Tío* Jesús in Kansas City. Long, backbreaking
excursions in the fields were conveniently transformed
into exotic trips to Mexico. And my summer vacation was
just another three months to make up the best bullshit
story ever!

As an English-speaking coconut, I longed for the
picture-perfect *gabacho* (Anglo-American) vacation that
every Mexican-American deserves. Disneyland would

have been perfect, but I would have settled for a trip to the ocean or any of the many American theme parks.

I grew up on the west side of town, which was known for its gang and also the animals, which outnumbered people two-to-one. Most of these creatures resided in houses that were located to the west of the railroad tracks and on the north side of East Zenos Road. Mrs. Mazón to the east was the Goat Queen of the *barrio* having more than thirty in her backyard. But no one else in the neighborhood even came close to our variety and number of animals. We definitely gave the San Diego Wild Animal Park a run for its money, especially since our park was for free. *Gratis.*

We had everything from horses, goats, cows, pigs, ducks, doves, and pigeons to rabbits, guinea pigs, peacocks, dogs, cats, and exotic birds. We swapped, traded, sold, gave, and inherited animals on what seemed a daily basis. One of our most unforgettable animals was a half-blind horse given to us for free and described to my father as being "great with kids." My father was not told that this nameless horse was only good with kids while it was eating. However, when the horse was done, it had no problem biting, kicking, or farting on anyone in its way or on its back. After a couple of months of near fatalities, my father decided to give it away to another horse-loving *familia* with lots of kids.

Animals were always at the center of the commotion at our house. Cows, chickens, pigeons, and rabbits were staples in our diet. My father would be extremely selective about an animal's appearance before deciding whether it should be eaten. This included the fancy rabbits that we purchased in a pet store in Washington State and brought back home in a cage, only to be eaten a few weeks later. Needless to say, my father was an animal lover, and there were no critters more cared for and revered than his colorful fighting roosters. The care that he bestowed upon them was superb. They ate nothing but the finest grains, which were part of a balanced diet. They were exercised regularly and given periodic medical checkups, especially before an upcoming tournament.

My father was a cockfight fanatic. He seemed to incarnate himself into every *gallo* (rooster) that ever stepped into the fighting arena. They were an extension of his ego, his personality, and his unaccomplished, unsettled dreams. Putting on his *gallero* (cockfighter) outfit always transformed him into the other *him*, the seemingly invincible, proud person he wanted to be.

Luck, however, has always been a cockfighter's worst enemy, bringing defeat to even the most cared for cocks and emptying even the best gambler's pockets. My father was on a mission to be the best *gallero* this side of the Mexican and Arizona borders and knew that someday his name would bring fear to every opponent when the line was drawn for the next fight. For years, however, the only thing that my father gained was a meager reputation and a hell of a lot of excuses to party, since winning, as well as losing, was always a reason to party.

Through the years, the few winnings were offset by the many losses, and eventually cockfighting evolved into a Vegas-style addiction, though without the dazzling lights or glamorous showgirls, yet with the much-needed trips back in search of a lucky win.

Cockfights have always been illegal in California, at least for as long as I can remember, but it doesn't mean that they didn't occur. They were just strategically planned underground, and events were moved one step ahead of the local authorities. Somehow the word would get around in the cockfight circles about the next big event, even if it took place in another state. Summerton, Arizona, was one of the popular places, as it provided reasonable access for many diehard *galleros* from this side and that side of the borders. Trips to the *palenques* (cockfight tournaments) depended on the physical condition of my father's roosters as well as the number on our farm. Nevertheless, there was never a shortage of cocks that were willing and ready to fight.

We usually left our house for the tournament late Friday afternoon or early Saturday morning after the crowing of the anxious roosters. Their wake-up calls announced to everyone the beginning of our cockfight vacation, as all thirteen family members plus two or three prized cocks boarded our brown cage on wheels. My unwillingness to go along was transformed into jubilation when I realized that I wouldn't be working in the fields this particular weekend.

The trip seemed to last forever as we traveled to an unappealing destination to take part in an illegal and immoral sporting event. Our arrival at the sport complex was welcomed by anxious onlookers waiting to get a glimpse of the competition, pretending to look busy as they exercised their cocks for all to view. While my father and brothers unloaded the cages, I would take advantage of my father's current high and ask him for some money, which would provide me with the necessary junk food for the entire weekend.

As the fights started, I would find myself in the stands looking down and wishing I was somewhere else—to be someone else. Bored and frustrated with the senseless massacre of the beautiful feathered creatures, I would exit quickly and circle the fighting arena. With each pass I would notice the growing number of dumpsters filled with dying cocks and would watch in amazement as they continued to battle even to their last breath, collapsing into a stiff fighting stance for the very last time.

The cockfights would continue throughout the afternoon and eventually the men and the animals were given a break late in the evening to have their wounds cared for and to count their winnings and their losses.

In the morning, we would wake to the noise of injured cocks and anxious fighters ready to resume their bloody sport. Stretching and fighting off the sleep, our stiffened bodies would slowly unfold from their sitting positions in the car, and we would wander into the cold morning air to look for breakfast and a much-needed bathroom. As the tournament resumed its crazed atmosphere, the division between the winners and the losers became increasingly apparent; their faces showed their joy and anger. If my father was lucky, one of his prized cocks would make it to another round, giving him a false sense of hope that would ultimately be spoiled by defeat.

After we had packed our Suburban with empty cock cages and empty spirits, we would start on our way home, and the entire process would start all over again. Along the way, my father would complain about the referees and the bad calls they made, swearing to come back soon and teach everyone a championship lesson.

Nearing our home, I would begin to mentally flip through my files to ensure that my new vacation story hadn't already been presented by me or someone else. I often debated on whether or not to tell the truth. However, no one would ever believe my cockfight vacation, yet everyone would definitely believe my meeting with Mickey.

The Punch

$\mathcal{M}$ost of my life's greatest disappointments have been simple ones. For example, the day that my first real girlfriend left me for another *vato* (dude) because he had a nicer car, the day I had to replace my entire eight-track tape collection for trendier cassettes, and the day we drove into a workcamp in Planada, *Califas*. Not that any other camp was any better, but this place reeked with familiar disappointment even though it looked more like a small town than a camp. Its never-ending shacks and matching work vehicles stretched for miles. It was located in the heart of the boonies. The noise and energy of the camp were muffled by the vigilante fig trees that periodically shed purple tears for their caretakers. Our first day at the camp brought the usual awkwardness of not knowing anyone and not knowing which way was north. After disinfecting our new cabin, we took a much-needed break and found some comfort in the setting sun.

In the morning our makeshift town provided the familiar urban sounds of turning engines, morning wake-up calls, and bilingual radio stations playing their musical specialties. We ended up in Planada after leaving Washington State because of a disappointing berry season that provided us with only enough money to cover what we spent on groceries. It had been an extremely wet year that had kept us indoors for most of the picking season. It had left us with nothing but time for the art of gambling and for mastering the Ouija board.

In Washington, the relentless rain had damaged most of the farmers' crops that summer but had done wonders for retail plastic sales. In hopes of cheating Mother Nature, workers outfitted themselves with plastic rain gear that looked as bad as it worked. Working on our knees was all that the rain needed to sneak cold water into our field scuba gear and eventually soak us. The chilly water turned our *calzones* (underwear) into soggy rags. As we dug our knees deeper into the pasty earth, our *nalgas* (behinds) turned into giant brown raisins.

Our bad plastic investment and the cold weather that made us hungry played havoc with the family's piggy bank. The weather was not getting any better, and we watched our family's savings dwindle down to what we had started with, so we decided to migrate back to

California in search of better pickings. Planada was described to my father as a gold mine in the heart of the golden state. We were promised a place to stay and never-ending labor to satisfy our appetite for work. However, all we found was fool's gold in the scorched fields, toasted to a golden brown by the unmerciful sun which reached orgasm by 10:00 a.m. We had missed most of the earlier crops, and with the endless supply of hands provided by the makeshift city, it was no surprise that there was not as much work as others had said. So we took the first job that came our way, and we found ourselves picking green tomatoes for fancy dinner salads.

I was the youngest of the legal pickers in my family, but I barely met the law's requirement. Even if I hadn't, my fate would have still been the same. We were working by the hour, filling large, green-stained buckets that once had been white. We had never done this kind of work before, so we had failed to buy the much-needed rubber gloves to protect our hands from the abrasive leaves and thorny weeds that protected their territory. On that first day, our hands turned to a Hulk green, and our bodies turned limp and heavy while we continued on with our monotonous work.

As a twelve-year-old child, I felt that my young mind should not be wasted on such a simplistic task. Therefore, I decided to challenge myself and find a creative solution to my suffering. I had to come up with something that was precise, sneaky, and flawless in order to grant me the freedom that I desperately sought. Looking back into my parents' tired faces, I was reminded of their gullibility for cheap wrestling and Mexican B movies. The answer had been under my nose all along; it was revealed to me by my merciful imagination. I was convinced that by faking the beginning of a heatstroke my parents would release me from my duties. It would work if I gave an Oscar-winning performance.

I held my breath to bring some redness to my face. Next, I focused on my green fist that would deliver the freedom punch. As I closed my eyes, my nose acted like a magnet. My fist struck the target with complete accuracy. With a numb face, I quickly cupped my hand under my nose, waiting the arrival of the sacrificial blood. The warm liquid mixed artistically in my green-stained hands, forming an indigenous brown paste.

Feeling a lot like De Niro in *Raging Bull* but looking more like a true Aztec warrior, I lunged forward, displaying my bloody face to my parents who reacted with horror and concern. Never before had I received such royal treatment. I was diagnosed by my parents as having a heatstroke and was ordered to sit under a tree, courtesy of a nearby almond orchard. I was given a wet rag to cover my nose and to wipe away the dry blood that

decorated my face. But like a true warrior I refused to rid myself of the markings that spoke of my bravery while fighting the sun. I held my head back in defiance and celebrated my triumph over a demeaning situation.
I smiled.

It wasn't long before my imagination asked me for a payback. I began to scribble on the ground with a stick, content to be doing what I loved: drawing, thinking, and relaxing. A couple of hours passed while drawing after drawing was erased from my endless earth pad. I cleared an even bigger area for my ultimate earth mural.

Preparing for this next challenge, I cautiously looked toward my parents and panicked when I saw my mother stumbling across the rows, making her way toward me. Seeing this, I quickly resumed my acting role. I slumped over my knees and hid my face between my legs, delivering another one of my monster Hulk jabs, reopening the blood dam. As the warm blood dripped out, my imagination couldn't pass up such a creative situation. I began bombarding some ants on the ground, knocking the food out of their mouths, and giving them a brand-new paint job. By the time my mother arrived there was no doubt in my mind that I had delivered another Oscar-winning performance.

Strawberry Face

A smack upside the head woke me from my climactic dream and along with it faded my twelve-year-old erection. Again, I had failed to mechanically pick all of the strawberries on both sides of the rows. This had not gone unnoticed by the field foreman, who was onto me. I had no excuse for what I had failed to do, and even if I did, the field was no place for it.

My imagination had once again been put on hold and now I was faced with an impossible predicament. I was to provide my father and the foreman with a miracle. You see, I was the weak piston in the Silva picking machine, and somehow I was not in sync with the rest of the family. Maybe it was my attitude or possibly my lack of etiquette in the field. It could never have been my age. Besides, what would a twelve-year-old *mocoso* (snotty kid) know anyway?

My father's snarls and threats added more weight to
my already fragile and tired body. He warned me for the
last time about the consequences of future missed
strawberries. When he walked away, I concentrated on
my rebellious picking hands that ignored my every
command and in return flipped me off for being scared.

My evil twin who lived in the back of my mind
reminded me that he was sick and tired of being pushed
around. He was ready to make the hit and put away
anyone who stood in our way! I shook him away allowing
my imagination to reenter and console me, reminding me
of the temporary nature of my situation. The twin rushed
back in to mock us both telling me I was living a foolish
dream, a dream that would never come true. He pointed
out the reality I was living, saying I didn't need to put up
with anymore demeaning situations like this one. I cut
him off and shut him up by humming "Dream Weaver."

As I fought to keep control, I cursed everyone
responsible for my predicament while I continued picking
every damn strawberry in sight. Fighting back the sissy
tears, I programmed myself on autopilot, knowing that
what I needed was an unemotional, and unimaginable
state of mind.

My desperate attempt to conform now seemed to be
under complete control. I had managed to become numb
to the whole situation, that is until a voice thundering from

above forced me to look up. In a slow-motion sequence, I was put back to artificial sleep as my eyes closed against the bloody strawberries that were smashed against my face.

A warm trail of fake blood trickled down my soiled chin as I tried to make sense of what had happened. My evil twin screamed the hideous crime he was about to commit. Simultaneously, my imagination desperately worked on regaining control and took me away once again to paradise.

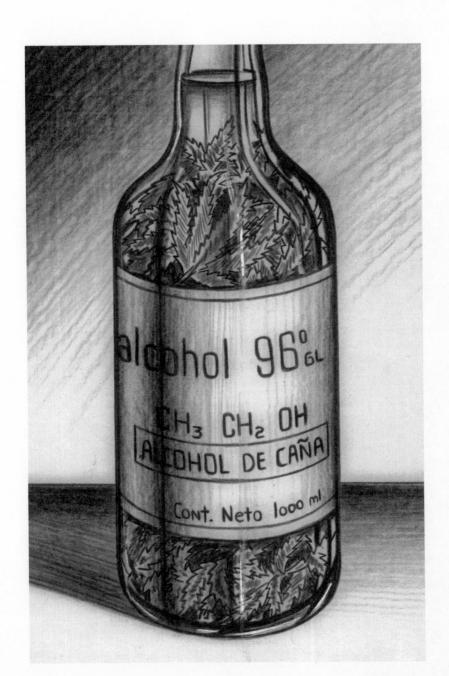

The Ultimate Home Remedy

I can count on one hand the number of times that our family visited the doctor. Even prior to my earthly existence, hearsay has it that home remedies cured all of my family's ailments. Doctors were hired only for "real emergencies" and even then a bartering system was always used for services rendered. The delivery of my two oldest siblings was paid for with healthy animals, and the same was done for my brothers and sisters who followed. However, the payment always varied since it depended on the animals we had in stock.

Because of a lack of funds and no health insurance, the word *emergency* had an ambiguous definition in our house. It wasn't until my femur had been separated for several hours that my father and uncle decided my "sprained" leg might actually be a serious fracture. On another occasion, several home remedies were used on my youngest brother before his ruptured appendix was finally attended to by a physician.

It is a true miracle that our fatality rate has remained at zero percent. One possible explanation for our mind-baffling survival might be the strict enforcement against food mixing. This family practice eliminated the possibility of food poisoning by making sure that things such as watermelon and milk, lemon and milk, hot and cold, or old and new were not put combined to form a volatile mixture. Another lifesaving factor might have been the herbs that were used to cure our Mexican ailments. For example, a piece of *ruda* (rue) in the ear was used to cure a throbbing earache. Another popular treatment was a body massage with a potion made of alcohol and marijuana for aching bones or the common cold. A touch of saliva was applied on our ears before we entered the water. And, of course, *té de manzanilla* (chamomile tea) provided relief for an upset stomach.

Minor operations were also performed on a regular basis, causing future patients to hide their pain. It was common for a piece of glass to be removed from the foot by the family's "head surgeon" while his loyal assistants held the patient over the bathtub. All of this of course was done without the benefit of anesthesia or money. A deep gash on the side of my stomach that normally would have required stitches was taken care of with a miracle-inducing Scooby Doo or Batman Band-Aid.

Our family's migrations put us in the most interesting and unusual circumstances, which challenged our arsenal of home remedies. Their curative powers came in handy whenever someone fell off a ladder while picking peaches or when a can full of cucumbers clobbered someone on the head. They also provided relief for the irritation caused by ingrown hairs on our knees that were aggravated by kneeling during work. Heatstrokes, muscle spasms, scratches, and sprained muscles were also cared for with our home remedies.

However, nothing compares to the ultimate home remedy invented by my father during our stay at a labor camp in Washington State. This camp consisted of a group of shacks built out of quarter-inch plywood walls, tin roofs, and makeshift beds. No one knew exactly how old these dwellings were, but I'm sure that carbon dating on the old, stained mattresses would reveal some history worthy of scientific research. These mattresses were historical accounts of what they had endured during their lifetimes. Through the process of aging, they had developed a self-protection mechanism that repelled human beings, as well as small rodents, by emitting foul odors and displaying grimacing faces outlined in yellow stains. In addition, each mattress had a life of its own and provided *piojos* (lice) with cheap and abundant territory.

Our beds were the most important commodity during our stay, second only to the propane stove in our cabin. The pain brought upon by twelve or fifteen hours of backbreaking work could only be neutralized through deep sleep on our prehistoric mattresses. These untamable mattresses fought off our weight as they bulged in several places, displacing our tired and aching bodies. Lucky for us, our fatigue was all the anesthesia necessary to ignore anything but sleep.

It took us only a few days to realize that once again we had been invaded by *piojos* while we slept. We found ourselves furiously scratching our heads and for a moment forgetting about our aching bodies. In a military-style inspection, we stood in line clawing at our scalps and dreading the all-too-familiar consequence. The discovery of the invaders called for our heavy-duty home remedy. We were ordered to stand in line outside our cabin and to strip to the waist. Next we had to close our eyes and hold our breath while we prayed for a quick and painless deliverance. As the spray penetrated our hair, the excess liquid formed into tiny rivers that cascaded off our ears to our bare shoulders and eventually down our backs. We were told to maintain our position so that the remedy would search out and destroy the enemy. Meanwhile, we battled to wipe away the excess before the burning liquid reached our shut eyes.

My brothers and I were always the first to hit the front lines followed by my hysterical sisters who refused the remedy. To them, the possibility of hair loss was a greater concern than the embarrassment caused by curious onlookers. Like all tragedies of war, no one was immune, and my sisters eventually made their way to the front. As each took her turn, she stood there momentarily, glaring a tearful eye at the can of Raid.

The Graduation Gift

*G*rowing up in Holtville I experienced my share of small-town disasters such as the cancellation of the world-famous Carrot Parade because of possible sabotage by labor union extremists. Another time of crisis was when the digital clock that faced the town park became unreadable because too many light bulbs had burned out, and nobody bothered to replace them for months. We never knew if it was 3:00 or 8:00.

In the Valley, I had experienced a number of dramatic upsets. For instance, the Holtville Viking football team beat *Calecia* (Calexico, California) for the first time in school history. Also, it was a shock to find out that *Q-VO* magazine had selected a half-white chick for the *Ruca Más Suave Del Año* (finest chic of the year).

All of these disasters were overshadowed by the announcement of a national gas shortage during which there was strict rationing of gasoline. My reasons for concern differed from those of most of the country's economists in that I feared the possibility of rioting by addicted cruisers like myself who had a craving for their daily trips to El Centro.

The year was 1979, and I had reached my lower threshold of educational maturity, which was and still is a major accomplishment for a small-town browny. I was a graduating senior with serious concerns about my future education. However, I decided to work on one thing at a time and that one thing happened to be my graduation celebration.

For all seniors, this major accomplishment brought the required gifts that varied depending on how much money your parents had. The rich *ranchero* kids were given lavish European vacations. The middle-class kids received brand-new cars given to them a few weeks prior and that might still be intact. The bottom-feeders, well, their gifts could range from a well-planned *pachanga* (party) to a shopping spree at Las Palmas, the Valley's hippest swap meet. I did not fit into any of these categories. I was in a gift category all by myself. I was in the *unknown* category, which meant that my gift could be Old Spice cologne to anything made by Fruit of the Loom. However, if I was really lucky it would be a crisp new twenty-dollar bill.

The Santa Ana Winds historically came uninvited to all of the high school graduation ceremonies and did their part in causing havoc with the caps, gowns, and skirts. As I dressed for my two minutes of fame, I couldn't help but focus on the celebration that would follow. I hadn't been invited to the best graduation parties, but that had never stopped anyone from crashing them, including myself.

Before leaving for the ceremony, my celebration came to a grinding halt as my *jefa* (mother) handed me a verbal pregraduation gift. It was described to me as a red-eye, one-way trip to McMinnville, Oregon, a nonrefundable ticket that guaranteed me a front-row seat aboard the Brown Bomber Express. At a Mach-three speed everything that I had looked forward to, like the congratulatory hugs, the champagne and beer, and the sweet sound of party music, all vanished into thin air. My mother cautioned me to report back two hours after the ceremony or I would be considered AWOL.

My enthusiasm and happiness had fallen victim to fool's gold syndrome, a seasonal virus that affected thousands of migrant families every summer. Unwilling to face graduation without a celebration, I contemplated running away. Ultimately, my conscience drove me home to prepare for my ordeal north. I viciously began packing my aging *calzones* (underwear), along with my best working clothes into a heavy-duty trash bag that couldn't possibly hold my heavy dilemma.

As we drove out of our driveway, we maintained the lead position in a three-car caravan that included the Partida and the Guerrero families. I found myself drinking my tears as we passed by *Brole* (Brawley, California) at 10:30 p.m. I checked my heart for fatal injuries. The darkness and complete silence nurtured the growing thoughts that were slicing through my mind and piercing my leaders in the back.

At this point of the trip my *jefe* (father) said that we were running late, and he sped trying to catch up to an imaginary shadow of where we should be. We continued on Highway 86, which had gained the reputation of being the killer highway, a term that appealed to me greatly at the moment. My anger helped block out the foul smell of the eighty-nine octane gasoline that permeated the van. Fearing that the restriction of gas sales would affect our trip's progress, *los tres jefes* (the three leaders) had decided to each buy two five-gallon containers, which were carefully packed into the back of each van. This ingenious idea transformed our vans into traveling time bombs, activated for self-destruction.

As we neared the town of Thermal, California, we noticed a distant flickering flame illuminating our destination. It rapidly magnified itself as we neared our target and was transformed into a giant flamethrower, spitting fire viciously as it was cheered on by the Santa Ana winds. The packing shed off the side of the highway was completely engulfed in flames, taunting us to come closer.

Defeat was something that only God could point out to our three fearless leaders as they conducted an off-the-road powwow. At this point, we needed a powerful rain dance, but it was unknown to these chiefs. Giving up on their mortal powers, they decided to have faith on an even greater gift of theirs: their arrogance. They decided to kamikaze straight through the fiery blockade and pray for the best.

Back on the highway, our traveling gas chamber had miraculously transformed itself into St. Simon's Cathedral, where the heavy-duty religious artillery was about to be unleashed for protection. The fail-safe *rosario* (rosary) that once lay next to the Max Factor lipstick in my *jefa's* purse now served as a tourniquet around her calloused fingers. A warrior-like drumbeat filled the confined space as my father pounded spiritual life into his chest. I continued with my blasphemous thoughts that found themselves in a battle of good versus evil.

Before facing death, I made one last attempt at asking myself some of my life's most important questions: How could I not be adopted? How could my life be fair? Who would I be dancing with right now? What is Europe like?

What would my own brand-new car smell like? What does it feel like to make love? Who would I have married? Would Elvis still be king if he was black? I knew that none of this really mattered and that I didn't matter either. If I did, wouldn't I be sipping champagne as my parents wiped away tears of pride and overwhelming happiness? Maybe blowing up on Highway 86 wasn't such a bad idea after all. It would definitely put me out of my misery. After some thought, I welcomed the idea of exploding into thin air and becoming one with my *calzones*, along with my work clothes and the greasy Teflon frying pans rattling in the back.

As the scorching heat pounded our wagon, the flames illuminated our firey figures onto the front windshield. My *jefa* clutched her *rosario* in her right hand and prayed for strength to fight in future battles. For a brief moment, my father pleaded for salvation while forcefully pounding his chest. A moment later he changed his mind and wished for life to continue our hopeless journey for gold.

I held my gaze in the glass for a moment or two, and prayed that this was just another bad dream.

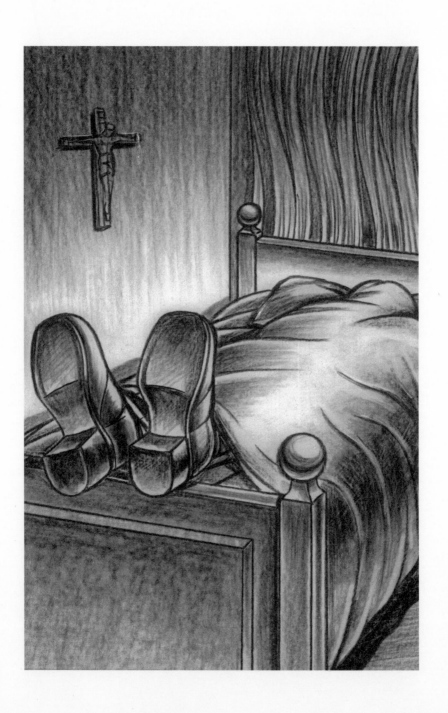

The Day My Brother Died

*T*he day my brother José died came as no surprise to us since we had all voted him as the sibling most likely to die first. We all referred to him as Crazy José, and we weren't all that proud of him. My mother claimed that his insanity was the result of an unpaid *manda* (religious promise), and my father's theory was that it must be a genetic problem because José seemed to take after my *Tío* Miguel. On the other hand, I believed that, unfortunately, he had been dropped at birth on the wrong side of the border. I knew this to be true because of his extremely flat ears that hugged his head in an aerodynamic fashion.

He had an American craziness about him; always dissecting perfectly good radios, televisions, and clocks for no apparent reason. We knew that death by electrocution was a possibility as was death at the hands of an outraged sibling who had found José in the front yard raking leaves or practicing mechanics while wearing someone else's new clothes. Regardless of the infinite possibilities, José seemed to take his role rather seriously, going out of his way to prove his insanity. I believed his paranoia made him feel important because it provided him with an audience for his never-ending stunts.

He was also a product of the seventies, which offered him a smorgasbord of drugs to further his experiments and take his nonconformist behavior to the next level. It was during one particularly bad trip that he reached a maximum state of insanity. Also at this point he began sending off for every popular TV game show contestant form available. *Jeopardy*, *Name That Tune*, and *The Price Is Right* were all going to retire his jersey and give him a place in the game show hall of fame. Before leaving high school, he left his mark by joining the prestigious Holtville High School Marching Band of Pride only to quit the day of his first public appearance, claiming that the tuba just wasn't his style.

The arrival of disco was the long-sought-after aphrodisiac as he went on a polyester-and-elevator-shoe craze. Once he even claimed that he had lost a major dance competition because Elsa, his dance partner, had failed to appropriately shave her armpits. The triple spin move that led him under her right armpit was spoiled by the confrontation with her overgrown, dangling hairs.

With the passing of disco, José used his newfound talent for dance at his new jobs, dancing from one to the next, always claiming boredom or poor management for his resignation. His seemingly never-ending list of jobs kept us all thinking he might be striving to break into the *Guiness Book of World Records*, or perhaps he was just being thoughtful toward us, since we visited him for free merchandise at every new location.

Along with picking up the nasty habit of stretching the truth, he also began the practice of moving his finger in the air as if to be figuring out complex math calculations. Shaving his head clean also became another one of his trademarks. So when he started the hyperventilation attacks that drove him into a frenzy, we accepted it as another one of his crazy antics. The countless trips back and forth to the hospital, however, proved us all wrong and made us wonder if we weren't all going crazy with him.

The useless doctors tried to end his attacks with paper bags, and my mother took him on countless trips to the *curanderos* (folk healers), but it all proved to be in vain. The battles between my parents over his condition didn't make things any easier for us. My father claimed that it was all part of a mischievous scheme on my brother's behalf.

If José wasn't born crazy, I am sure that our house
had all the right ingredients for producing hallucinations.
The weekend parental clashes that left us wetting our beds
at night were probably one of José's favorite evening
shows.

José had managed to keep his job picking carrots
longer than any other, and he took great pride in being one
of the best at his craft. He had also been consistent in his
work habits to the extent that it impressed my father
tremendously. The wake-up call that my father bellowed
out one morning was not heard by anyone but myself, and
it reminded me of my luck. Fifteen minutes had passed as
I woke once more to the second and final wake-up call,
which became louder as my father approached José's bed.
It was at this point that my eyes exploded wide open in
horror and glared at the blanket that covered my brother's
still body. My father made several desperate attempts at
bringing José back. His piercing shrieks that called out
for help lifted the hair on my back and drove me to seek
comfort in a curled-up fetal position. Everyone took turns
at shaking his limp body, blasting their cries to maximum
levels, and refusing to believe that he was gone.

The slow and delayed movements that eventually
followed were a miracle to all as José began to mumble
something about being okay. None of us had ever
welcomed one of José's crazy stunts as much as this one,

because this one had brought him back from the dead. The truth was that the valium which had been prescribed to him over the years had given him an addiction in place of a cure, and the result had been a near overdose.

As I lay there intently looking for signs of José's breathing, I thought about the effects of a near death in the family and all of the other traumatic experiences that were a regular part of our household. I began to see that José wasn't crazy at all. Instead, I believed he was just trying to cope with the insanity that surrounded our daily lives. He just seemed to handle it in his own unique way.

Ode to a Cholo

I often wonder what happened to my other high school classmates, in particular those who I vaguely knew and who were voted most likely to fail. Students who were thought of as lacking a sense of direction yet who had enough pride to go beyond most of our expectations. Persons labeled "troublemakers," "nonachievers," and left to fend for themselves, never given the least amount of thought as to their integral role in the system of things.

The person who comes to mind, who was without a doubt the most infamous of all, is Federico, alias "El Gato." He was a slow-talking, slow-walking *vato* who made the tardy roll four years running. He was a tall, slender fellow who was rarely seen without his slick black hat, spit shiners, and patented creases that accentuated his graceful cat walk.

Aside from his clean outfit, El Gato was known to carry all of his six sweethearts on his right arm. Five of them had been crossed off with scars in order to maintain accurate inventory and to keep his current *jaina* (girlfriend) happy.

It was known that El Gato came to school with more accessories than Ken and Barbie ever had. Adding to his cool stride was a cane carved out of mesquite that was used for more than just a walking companion. It was an accessory that was always confiscated at the front office and held there for security reasons. He added another notch to his stick after any *pleito* (fight), a ritual he described as the adding of another *marca* (mark).

A long silver-plated chain was also a telling sign of El Gato's presence, an attention-getter that sparked interest as it scraped the ground he walked on. It was rumored that he had once attempted to wear the chain during his P.E. class in order to accentuate the mandatory green trunks and white sneakers.

El Gato was a bilingual kind of *vato* long before bilingualism became political; he said things like "I'll kick your *dona*," "Come here, *mi'jita*," or "*Trucha con el principal.*"

El Gato was feared by all, liked by most, and eyed by all the *chicas*, which gave him a reputation in and out of the fighting circles.

He claimed he was the hottest ride in town, offering all the *chicas* a free ticket.

El Gato was from the center of town, which left him without a gang to side with, so he became the sixth man to all the gangs in town, filling in where he was needed most. Even though Holtville had its share of gangs, for the most part all of the members were pretty harmless. Most of the *chingasos* (blows) were white on brown or brown on white depending on who threw the first blow. Like any other young person with a label, he was stereotyped and viewed as a threat not because of his juvenile record, but because of his impressive attire.

Through the years El Gato made several attempts to blend in. One of these attempts was enrolling his car, known as "*La Flaca,*" into the local lowrider car club known as the "Low Impressions," that was previously known as the "Slow Temptations" and six months earlier had called themselves the "Latin Cruisers." He had also joined the high school basketball team, but eventually he was dropped from the team because of his lack of hustle and the amount of technical calls that he picked up for fighting with opposing players and referees.

Most of El Gato's free time was spent cruising with his homies: El Maya, El Bigface Carotas, La Wina, El Perro y El Tweety. He also attended car shows and occasionally got rowdy across the border.

41

It's pretty clear as to El Gato's *placaso* (nickname), and it was also common knowledge as to his rough childhood. Living in a small town forced private matters to become public news especially when the *chisme* (gossip) hit the *comadre* circuit. It was said that his *jefes* had divorced when he was six years old, and in the process his mother picked up a *padrastro* (stepfather) who couldn't stand to see him, *ni pintado*.

Growing up under these circumstances, El Gato progressively spent more and more time with other kids just like him, always keeping his mind occupied and looking for ways to nurture his pride.

In high school the nonachievers were separated from the other students by a process of isolation. The shop students were pushed one way, and the college-bound ones were pushed another. During this time, El Gato roamed the halls as a vigilante of sorts, always looking out for his *raza* when push came to shove, clearing the path for those of us who had been told that we had a chance at making it in life. He was always ready to make the hit on the person who was trying to put the few of us down, sacrificing himself and giving us the peace of mind that someone was watching over us.

Wrestling Match
at Midnight

Through the years our home provided us with ringside seats to numerous, untelevised fighting events. These bouts between my mother and father delivered a sucker punch that would later instill a blind and desperate love in the hearts and minds of my sisters. The result would be a distorted perception of what a normal relationship between a husband and wife should be.

Even the odds in Vegas could never have been this bad considering the selection of my sisters' marital matchups. The gambling done by my sisters won me a group of legally binding *cuñados* (brothers-in-law) that gave a precise definition to the word *pendejo* (idiot). The champion of this embarrassing bunch of fools was Animal Andre, the biggest *pendejo,* whose stupidity was equal in stature to that of the infamous King Kong. He was a former high school football star who displayed as much style as a heavyweight wrestler wearing spandex. His goals in life were even less impressive. They were driven by a slow-moving ambition to party and find the ultimate high.

Animal Andre's lack of respect for women was uncovered during a mismatched fight with my sister. The outcome left my sister in a black-and-blue condition that would make any ringside doctor wince with horror. There were numerous matches and rematches throughout my sisters' marriages because they were unaware of their well-ingrained addiction to the sport.

I grew up with a love for wrestling, admiring the showmanship and athleticism displayed by my favorite *luchadores* (wrestlers). Black Gorman, Mad Mountain Mike, *Mil Máscaras* (One Thousand Masks), Blue Demon, and Sonny Warcloud were just a few of my childhood heroes. They represented *lucha libre* (wrestling) at its best before it was tainted by capitalism and a flood of unmasked, obese wrestlers.

My favorite lethal move had always been *la patada voladora* (the flying kick), which was initiated with a running start and ended with a flying kick to the body. Most of the time it knocked the opponent to the ground, leaving him in position for the final count. Feeling the need to perfect my technique, I found it convenient to practice on my younger and fearless brotherly rivals, which gave me an undefeated record that still stands today. I knew that I had mastered my skill when I nearly knocked out my younger brother's lower tooth, an incident that was covered up with the aid of a monetary payoff.

Due to the financial burden brought upon by the increasing effectiveness of my flying kicks, I decided to stick to watching the sport that I loved. I felt honored to have witnessed the biggest upset in wrestling history as Black Gorman and his partner defeated Mad Mountain Mike in a hard-fought battle. It would seem that without actually witnessing this unprecedented account personally, one might consider me a liar. You see, Mountain Mike was big-real big. He was easily more than four hundred pounds. In all my years of watching professional wrestling I had never witnessed such a defeat, and it would inevitably be the powerful *patadas voladoras* that were administered to Mountain Mike in double doses that would leave him flopping on the canvas like a beached whale. I believed I had finally experienced the ultimate wrestling match, that is, until Animal Andre decided to show the world why he was king.

It was an off-season day that found my father returning from Mexicali where he had undergone an extensive tongue examination. It had consisted of a near tongue removal that left him speechless and extremely sore. The doctor prescribed painkillers that refused to take effect. Thus, a home remedy made from *pomada de la campana* (an ointment), *ruda,* and other secret herbs was concocted and rubbed along his neck in a nonstop, circular motion.

Nineteen seventy-four had been an injury-filled year and had produced the second fractured bone in my body. I had broken a fall with my right hand while attempting to retrieve my Mexican Frisbee, a plastic butter top that outperformed any Wham-O product. With two injured bodies in our household, my father decided to enact an early curfew at 7:30 p.m., which meant no talking, no moving, and no whispering. My sister had been dropped off at our house earlier and wasn't sure of the whereabouts of her wandering *pendejo.* It wasn't until 11:00 p.m. that the screeching tires announced to my sister that her prince charming had arrived safely. Animal Andre had been in training that evening and was not about to go home without a much-needed fight. He had chosen our arena solely because of the size of the crowd that was watching from a safe distance. Unfortunately, the match was cancelled since the parental referees refused to let such a mismatched bout ensue. Forbidden to display his talent, Animal Andre demonstrated his lack of sportsmanship by spitting and cursing at the crowd, vowing to return to pursue his fight. We hadn't been disappointed by Animal

Andre's performance, but what followed would
overshadow everything in past and present sports history.

We all decided to get some rest after Animal Andre's
departure. However, our adrenaline kept our hearts
pumping with excitement, enticing our minds to what
could have happened. Our short sleep came crashing
down along with our front door as Animal Andre made a
superstar entrance, blasting his enormous body through
our hardwood door. There was a mad dash as everyone
looked to reserve a front-row seat to the fight of the
century. Running into the arena, we were disappointed to
find that one of the wrestlers had been exchanged for
another. Filling in for my sister was my father in his
flashy *chones* (underwear).

Animal Andre had a Chinese chokehold around my
jefe's sore neck. My father desperately signaled with his
hands what appeared to be "help" in Spanish. The crowd
screamed in horror as they witnessed the beating being
handed to this defenseless man who apparently was no
match for Animal Andre's power. The compassion they
felt lead them to begin piling up on both wrestlers. As
bodies were slammed before my eyes, the entire arena
emptied its seats onto the ring, creating a blurred mass of
kicking legs and swinging arms. With no referee in sight,
the match continued into what seemed an eternity, with
disqualifying moves and cries for help. I looked down at

the cast around my broken arm that prohibited me from taking part in the defeat of Animal Andre. All I could do was stand there and look away in shame.

The $27.00 Experience

*B*uzzzzzzzz! Buzzzzzzzz! I didn't know whether
to crush or kiss my alarm clock for the wake-up call that
saved my life once again. It had all been a Chicano
dream, another reminder from my brain letting me know it
was still in charge. I gave myself the mandatory parts
check, which included a good scratch or two before I
continued on to the next stage of awakening.

The taste of cheap American beer lingered in my
mouth as I made my way to the bathroom. I found myself
trying to justify the taste by reminding myself that there
had to be something stronger than faith for my life's
problems. Once again, I promised myself not to go
cruising with Paco, especially during the week. Besides,
our intellectual cruising sessions had never led to any deep
problem-solving since we always ended up right back
where we started. Staring at the bathroom mirror, I knew

that I had to start searching elsewhere for better beer and for better answers.

My armpits were already telling me it would be another hot, August Valley day. I finished my bathroom ritual that would prepare me for another *campesino* battle with Mother Nature and headed out the door. It was 4:00 a.m. when I began my predawn journey through the streets of Holtville's west side, dodging nasty looks from the insomniatic *perros* (dogs) along the way. The Alfredo Flores cargo bus left punctually at 4:15 a.m., and it announced to the entire *barrio* that another day had begun.

Upon boarding the bus I selected a seat away from the chatterboxes and *pedorros* (farters). Mr. and Mrs. Chávez sat in the front of the bus as usual, sipping their coffee and complaining about their muscles or some newfound ailment. After saying "Good morning," I collapsed into my seat only to be shaken up by *Señor* Rodríguez, whose gut always entered the bus at least two feet ahead of him. Then came Mrs. Gómez whom I recognized by the smell of cheap perfume that only added to the carnival pungency already lingering in the bus. *Señorita* Méndez sat toward the front of the bus as well. She was the leftover of the litter and continued to cover her face for more than just working reasons. *Señor* García made several attempts at entering the bus through the rear while choking on his phlegm and passing gas. He made me wonder if anybody would knowingly administer mouth-to-mouth on him when his time was up. As he made his way down the aisle of the bus, he asked if anyone knew last night's scores, though never referring to any games in particular but hoping to start a conversation with anyone who was willing to listen. Finally, one of the last persons to board was Mr. Ramírez, who was mumbling the usual story about his wife making another attempt on his life by poisoning his *caldo* (soup) last night. However, the truth was he did not want to admit that he was just plain *crudo* (hungover) once again.

The bus took its course and I was knocked unconscious by the seat's punches, a beating I welcomed since this was the only way I could endure this kind of a trip. From the fringes of my sleep, I heard the *chisme* on herbal cures, upcoming concerts, championship wrestling, and secrets about people in our neighborhood.

Upon entering my first deep sleep, I was unwillingly transformed into a brown turtle that had been adopted by a chicken-shit family. All my energy centered around my burdensome, brown shell that was more embarrassing to me than my lack of speed. I knew that if I could only rid myself of this setback, someday I would be someone and prove it by giving the hare a legitimate rematch. In time, I managed to save enough money to have the surgical procedure that had been advertised as a cosmetic shell detachment. I was convinced that this and only this would transform me into the real me, the person who I truly was, and I would have the pink skin to prove it. Mr. García's continued phlegm battle provided the special sound effects that acted as the background for the cutting of useless nerves and tissue. The women's chatter added a sense of realism to the chain saw that finally detached my shell.

The operation was a complete success, and I was ready to prove it. I Fed Exed the hare immediately and challenged him to a race with no holds barred. We found ourselves at the starting line without having to wait for the promotional hype or the legalities of contracts. As we lunged forward at the crack of the starting gun, I came to a crashing halt, hitting the seat in front of me. The cheering of the crowd had actually been the shrieks of startled passengers. The bus had swerved to avoid hitting a rabbit that was crossing the road. Apparently, the starting gun I had heard was a giant backfire from the hole-riddled muffler. It was at this point of the trip that I braced myself for any further daring and unexpected maneuvers by Mr. Evil Kanevil Flores.

Our destination this day was a cotton field on the south side of the Salton Sea, a favorite destination of traveling tourists and migrating birds. As we neared the field, my eyes automatically collapsed shut and refused to allow any unpleasant images to enter. The $27.00 check that I would receive at the end of the day kept reminding me of why I was needed outside. We stumbled out of the bus like a group of Christians being led to the Colosseum, knowing how painful the detachment from being idle would be. We were handed our weapons to do battle: a couple of salt tablets and long-neck hoes that had more character than De Niro. Then we lined up like race horses at the Kentucky Derby, all in search of the finish line. Each passing of the cotton turnstiles seemed like an exact Xerox of the last. Meanwhile, we continued to rid the field of several types of unwanted, malignant growth. The thought of quitting consistently entered my mind and body two hours into the race. However, like a hypnotized rat led by the Pied Piper, we followed *Señorita* Méndez who blasted *cumbias* and *música ranchera* for all to hear. The day moved on, and we were steam-cooked like vegetables on a giant wok since the freshly irrigated field provided all the necessary moisture to keep us turning.

We entered our much-anticipated break at 9:00 a.m. with dry cotton mouths and newly dyed work wear. Apparently, we had overwatered ourselves with bleachy water. The soggy sandwiches and greasy *tacos* slowly brought some life back to our tired bodies, which inevitably the sun would steal right back. Reluctantly, we picked up our tools while the smart *huevones* (lazy ones) stretched their break by faking a quick run to the outhouse. Mr. and Mrs. Chávez, who every morning complained about their numerous ailments, seemed to have a miraculous remission in the intensity of their work. *Señor* Rodríguez was always handicapped by his enormous gut, which prevented him from efficiently eliminating all the weeds. Mrs. Gómez continued to take her vanity breaks, spraying another one of her many perfumes on a potential customer in hopes of making a sale. *Señorita* Méndez pissed everyone off again with the ridiculous pace she kept while working, leaving everybody to wonder about the possible use of steroids. *Señor* García seemed like he would make it through another day without choking on his phlegm, while *Señor* Ramírez spent a good part of the morning reminding Mr. Flores about his antidote for his wife's poison—a cold beer or two just to make sure.

Reaching the break point always gave us the hope of surviving the rest of the day, but this could not be accomplished without the arrival of our checks at eleven hundred hours. The frenzied finish was periodically spoiled by an occasional demand to finish a field or a heatstroke victim who had difficulty crossing the finish line. Our preparation for our trip back was always methodical, and it was completed with a roll call for the distribution of our big checks.

As we left the field, the hot August sun transformed

our bus into a Betty Crocker oven and cooked each of us to a golden brown until we were in great need of something cool. It was a tradition on the Flores Express to offer passengers the best treatment possible, which meant a pit stop at one of the many hidden country stores. Wong's Market was the habitual stopping place that offered the coldest beer in town. The proprietors were two old, fearless Chinese-Americans who spoke a Chinese cholo dialect and weren't the least bit alarmed by the entrance of our motley group. We made a mad dash that reminded me of pirates on a treasure hunt. The men scavenged for something alcoholic, while the women searched for a little excitement on the adult-magazine rack. The Wongs had a store policy to cash any check as long as it was used to purchase something in their store, even when the names on most of the checks failed to match those on people's IDs. Most of the people on the bus collected unemployment and so would transform themselves into their two-year-old kids or dead relatives. It was a harmless scheme that was welcomed by everyone involved.

The drive back would have made the KROQ party bus seem dull by comparison. The physical ordeal endured throughout the day was enough to give any man or woman enough pride to last for years. Therefore, the party bus heated up, and the men found themselves

sharing their prized alcohol while the women giggled at
the pages filled with hanging flesh that dangled before
their eyes. As the bus shifted gears, each conversation
grew louder, positioning for importance. Menus for
tonight's dinners were guessed on and wished for. Bets
were taken for every sporting event conceivable. And
there was much anticipation surrounding the next chapter
on the latest *novela* (soap opera).

The dust caused a commotion as the bus entered the
Alfredo Flores dirt parking lot, welcoming us home. Mr.
and Mrs. Chávez apologized for their quick departure and
explained to everyone the urgency to get home and start
their *marijuana-en-alcohol* therapy on their aching bodies.
As they left, *Señor* Rodríguez asked them for any leftover
tacos he could have. He needed them to counter the
effects of his upcoming alcohol binge. *Señorita* Méndez
was startled when she found herself holding the adult
magazine in her hands while Mrs. Gómez reminded her
about her Avon order, which was due tomorrow. *Señor*
García was busy passing his cap around asking for
donations to continue the party and asked Mr. Flores for a
ride into town. Mr. Ramírez suddenly found himself
feeling fully recovered and proved it to everyone left by
singing a potpourri of tragic *corridos*, shouting that his
death would someday inspire an equally great song.

By late afternoon, everyone that remained on the bus

had indulged in a blissful $27.00 experience. As I walked home, I stopped to say "hello" to the dazed neighborhood *perros*, telling them I would be seeing them again in the morning.

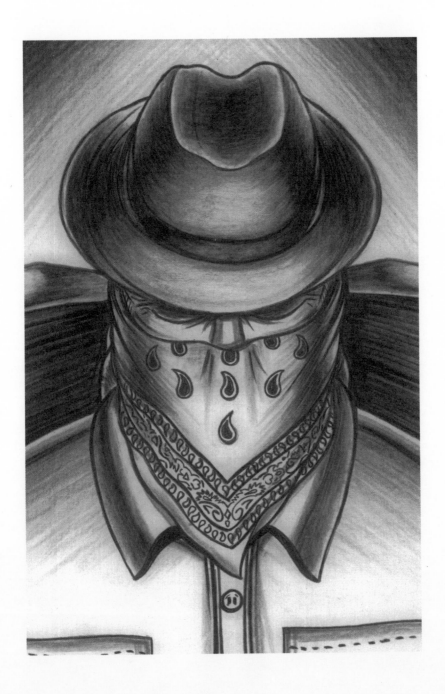

My Padrino Was
an Outlaw

*L*ong before news stations had sensationalized car chases involving crazy unknowns, I had already witnessed a real chase involving someone I knew. My *padrino* (godfather) Emilio was a full-fledged *macho* with the baddest *mostachón* (moustache) you will ever see. It was rumored that he had been on the run from Mexican authorities since the ripe age of seventeen, having single handedly put seven people into permanent sleep.

Nineteen seventy-eight was the first year that my *padrino* decided to try his luck *en el nuevo norte*. Packed with his faithful gun and *familia*, he waited outside our house for the arrival of the Guerreros to begin our unpredictable journey north.

After a full day of bologna sandwiches, gas refills, and stinky feet, we skidded into the nearest rest area for some much-needed rest. All three *familias* began pulling out their festive *cobijas* (blankets) to build our makeshift camp. We marked out our territory for the night between the dog-leash sign and the unused trash cans. As always, our sleep was disturbed by curious vacationers with spoiled, leashless dogs sniffing out the colorful cocoons that decorated the lawn. Sometime in the middle of the night most of us wandered back to our cars to sleep because we were sent back by annoyed parents or by the punctual sprinklers that whipped us into a frenzy.

I didn't know much about my *padrino* and what I did know came from rumors that floated around our *barrio* from one house to the next. Even as a fearless *hombre*, my *padrino* had a weakness. That weakness was an overpowering jealousy, a weakness that became evident as he stuck to his wife like a cold shadow. His jealousy was made extremely clear by the revolver that slept comfortably under his guarding ear.

Once we reached Oregon, our families lived in a secluded mountain house that provided a hideout for my *padrino*'s jealous ways. Our short stay in Oregon gave way to our new destination, as we found ourselves unpacking our belongings in a highly populated labor camp in Washington State with hundreds of curious onlookers. Although our families were in different camps, our new destination awoke in me a feeling that my *padrino*'s jealousy would be drawn out for all to see.

My *padrino*'s secret-service-style accompaniment of my *madrina* was noticed and respected by everyone, including me. However, my *madrina* constantly looked for the right moment to break away to find some privacy in her smothered life. Her moment came on a crab-hunting expedition by several families looking to add variety to our boring cuisine. While others looked for dinner, she took the opportunity to stroll along the endless beach and ended up at the state park restrooms. Unknowingly, my *madrina* had passed too close to someone of the opposite sex and in the process had acknowledged his presence with a friendly smile. From a distance my *padrino* watched as his anger rose with the rising tide, cursing himself for being distracted and disoriented by the elusive crabs. In a rage he cut through the waves that seemed to part in fear as they felt his angry stride, giving him a pathway to his wandering property.

Too many eyewitnesses detoured my *padrino* from acting out his fury. I knew that this would only inflame his anger. Collecting his belongings, he left looking for some privacy to display his rage.

The thin walls of their cabin seemed to amplify the shouting and the death threats for all the camp to hear. With his *cohete* (gun) at his side, my *padrino* kept his family's attention. He ordered them around from one room to the next while aiming his gun at each family

member. Caught in a life-and-death situation, my
madrina's motherly instincts gave her the will to protect
her *familia*, deciding to confront my *padrino* with words
of assertive force. At this point the alcohol, rage, jealousy,
and machismo forced my *padrino* to aim his weapon at
the woman he loved. As the unloaded weapon jerked back
and forth in slow motion, the victims jumped at the
opportunity to defend themselves. Even in his drunken
condition, my *padrino* held his ground using his calloused
fists to strike the young flesh, knocking each one of his
kind to the ground with great force. Looking for his gun,
he left a window of opportunity for his family to head out
the doors or smash the windows and jump to safety. Some
of them ran and hid in neighbors' cabins, while others,
more fearful, jumped across a canal to reach safer ground
in the raspberry fields that would protect them for the
evening.

While the family desperately ran, my *padrino* sat at
the front stairs of their cabin loading his gun, shouting for
them to return home. From a distance, young Tito's voice
could be heard saying, "*¡No, nos vas a matar!*" (No,
you're going to kill us!), while he ran away in search for
safety. My *padrino*'s response echoed in the night as he
shouted, "*¡Entonces los mato afuera!*" (Then I will kill
you outside!). After an unsuccessful search in the summer
night, my *padrino* roamed the camp, knocking on all the

doors and asking for his *familia* to be returned to him. Fearing his presence, lights went out and silence was everyone's response to the threats that grew louder into the evening. My *padrino*'s growing thirst eventually forced him to flee, vowing to return with more ammo and more beer. On his way back from town, he tired out, and instead of returning to the camp, he decided to park his van in the raspberry fields, sipping his beer and partying with Cornelio Reyna *y* Los Tigeres Del Norte.

The fear of a madman held the camp hostage, keeping everyone indoors throughout the evening and well into the morning. It wasn't until the field foreman arrived at the camp, wondering why no one had shown up for work, that people began coming out expressing their fear. After a hundred different interpretations of the incident, the foreman was able to piece together enough information for a police report. Suddenly, my *padrino* was one of the most-wanted men in the entire state of Washington.

It was late morning when my *padrino* awoke to the screaming sirens that crisscrossed the entire area, adding pain to his unbearable hangover. Instead of making an irrational decision, he decided to sleep it off and wait till sundown to plan his out-of-state getaway.

Rumors of the incident reached my family's labor camp by early afternoon, distorting the story's truth into a bloody scene. Everyone was at the camp's laundry room celebrating the birthday of Juan Ramírez, alias "La Muerte." Between the washers and the dryers we bumped and shook our booties to K.C. and the Sunshine Band, momentarily taking our minds off the terrible news. Only Juan Ramírez, the camp's oldest inhabitant, was worthy of such an extravagant celebration. The party soon came to a complete halt after an order was given by *Señor* Rogelio, the camp's caretaker. Juan Ramírez attempted to negotiate with *Señor* Rogelio and invited him to have a good time, pointing him in the direction of some lovely young girls. Refusing to be bribed, he began shaking his fists and his head, shouting at everyone to leave before he killed someone. Juan Ramírez calmly and politely asked everyone to leave, explaining that the party would continue later on that evening. All he needed was written permission from the Japanese owners, whom he knew very well. As the angry partyers exited, mumbled threats were made. *Señor* Rogelio stood at the front door, lock in hand, waiting to seal the dance hall. Juan Ramírez was last seen speeding down the camp's main drag, singing *"Volver Volver"* through his truck's intercom system. Everyone underestimated Juan Ramírez's chances to jump-start the party, so we all went to our cabins to sleep. Although the sun still stood high in the summer sky, we forced ourselves to fight off our adrenaline and set our mind on tomorrow's early rise. I went to bed thinking about the disbanded washroom party, but my main thoughts centered around my fugitive *padrino* and his unknown whereabouts.

Angrily I awoke in my darkened cabin after my exotic dream of Mexico was interrupted. Vicente Fernández became louder as I sat up in bed trying to figure out what was happening. The loud music echoed off the surrounding mountainsides, periodically interrupted by announcements of a continued Juan Ramírez fiesta. Like a mad ice cream man, he circled the camp, announcing through a loudspeaker his open invitation to all, expecting everyone to return and pick up where the party had stopped. The thought of an early-morning wake-up call kept everyone from returning, while a disappointed Juan Ramírez faded into the night.

At 10:30 p.m., a desperate knock again broke my sleep as I heard my father ask who it was. I heard my *padrino* identify himself in a timid voice, and ask if he could come in. We all climbed out of bed, taking turns peeking through the toilet-paper-filled holes that decorated our dividing wall. My *padrino* looked frail as I watched his hand tremble while he brought a beer to his lips. He explained to my father his version of the family incident and shared his plan to leave the state. Then, he asked my father for cash and another cold beer for the road. His best chance of escaping would be to travel at night, therefore he requested my father's advice about his premapped route. He asked for one last favor, making my father promise to look after his *familia* and his unused *cohete*. As we went back to sleep, we listened to his quick getaway into the night. I wondered if I would ever see my *padrino* again and about the possibilities of another dramatic wake up.

A short time passed when we again awoke to distant sirens speeding in our camp's direction. The slamming breaks and high-pitched screeching forced us out of bed. My father was the first to get up. I overheard him say that it looked like my *padrino*'s car, and he rushed to see if his *compadre* needed any help. We stood by the front door looking at the light show in the distance. My father's return only confirmed what we had expected. My *padrino* had been arrested and was on his way to the local county jail.

A screaming cell mate kept my *padrino* awake most of the night. Apparently, he had spent the evening trying to break his own arm by forcefully slamming it against the cell door. He had invited my *padrino* to join him in his escape plan, which would take place during their recovery at the local hospital.

The sobering power of the cell bars made my *padrino* decide to redeem himself through his one phone call to his wife. While on the phone, the once fearless man broke down, asking for forgiveness and begging for one last chance. He shared with his wife the enlightening experience that had taken place during the past forty-eight hours. Words that had been spoken before were uttered again, but this time they carried with them the promise of a changed man. The kids listened with apprehensive and doubting minds that had been scarred by broken promises of times past. My *madrina,* fearful of her newfound freedom, chose security under my *padrino*'s watchful eye.

Choco Milk and Other Revolutionary Drinks

Mexican drinks have always been at the forefront of trend-setting beverages. Long before flavored coffees were hip, Mexicans were spicing up their *cafecito* (coffee) with *canela* (cinnamon) or a nasal-opening *piquete* (shot) of tequila. For those of you looking for the cutting edge, look for Mexican drinks to deliver the key to being the baddest person of tomorrow, today! Be the first to have a vision of the future and a taste of the past.

It won't be long before beverage companies realize that the next trend will be *champurrado*, a warm, brown corn drink that wakes up the taste buds and nurtures the soul. Soon *champurrado* houses will replace coffee houses, and they will be the place to be seen, mingle, inspiring the next cultural revolution. Other beverages will follow since there happens to be no shortage in the variety of rich drinks available.

The new generation will be quenching their thirst with *horchata* while they cheer on the University of Aztlan to its first NCAA basketball championship. The sports stars of the future will be endorsing *Jamaica* Blast drinks, acknowledging the beverage as the force behind their fifty-plus-point games. *Cebada* will be the power drink of the first Mr. Chicano Universe and will sculpt amazing muscles reminiscent of a Mexican mountain range.

All 100% natural and 100% politically correct, these drinks will bring with them the spirit of our ancestors and the richness of our future. *Chocolate Abuelita* will bring humbleness and warmth to the hearts of many, and *cocos helados* (cold coconut drinks) will knock some sense into those who just don't get it.

My vision and respect for Mexican beverages came at a very early age as I was weaned on Choco Milk (we pronounced it *chocomeel*), the chocolate-flavored drink of the famous Pancho Pantera. He was a flying superhero panther who used his enriching powers to nurture cultural pride and political power.

Looking at a freshly prepared *tetera* (baby bottle) of Choco Milk brings tears to my eyes and warmth to my heart as I remember the magical powers derived from my childhood drink. It reminds me of the seven and a half years of continued nourishment provided by this famous powdered mixture. It was a drinking ritual that nurtured my imaginative mind and tenacious spirit, giving sustenance, value, and significance to the plastic container with an oversized nipple. The concoction would be scientifically prepared from a secret formula, creating a rich, brown liquid whirling in my glass like an untamable tornado ready to mix with the night's home-cooked dinner. It added a festive flavor to my meal, which consisted of *huevos estrellados, frijoles, y papas fritas* (eggs, beans, and potatoes).

Relishing my Choco Milk, I would hesitate between sips, making sure that there was enough left over for dessert. When the table had been cleared and the coast was clear, the precious liquid would be transferred to a green baby bottle with a large brown nipple. This dessert was much more than an after-dinner beverage. It was both soothing and refreshing. Its miraculous powers were essential for the development of my vision for the future as well as for the comfort of my soul.

When I was older running out of the school bus and straight into the kitchen became a ritual that I enacted to prepare my much-needed, therapeutic potion. Instead of the traditional couch and low-lit room, all I required was my Choco Milk and a thick, warm blanket that I used for comfort and security. It was my Chicano camouflage!

They say that you are what you eat, and I'm sure that

also means you are what you drink. Taking this into consideration, I would have to say that I happen to be a unique drink, rich with culture, and 100% Chicano-flavored.

The Last
Bachelor Summer

*T*he first close relative that I remember dying was my *Tío* José who passed away when I was in junior high school. As a result of this tragic experience, I developed an uneasy feeling about my mortality. Prior to my uncle's death, I had never given it much thought, except during moments of anxiety that surfaced whenever I encountered an overwhelming situation.

Most of us will not be remembered because, from a historical point of view, our lives are insignificant and invisible. If we're lucky we'll end up as a statistic worthy of news commentary. For example: Who exactly were the twelve undocumented workers who crashed off the 15 freeway last summer? Who was the woman who lost her life crossing the border yesterday? Who was the latest field worker to die of cancer?

Nineteen eighty-two brought me to another one of

these desperate situations. I had asked my parents for a
bigger share of my summer earnings, money that would
be used to pay for my outrageously high art-school tuition.
My desperate plea was answered with a flat refusal
delivered to me by my nervous mother. My hopes of
taking control of my future were spoiled, leaving me with
no other alternative than to go *solo para el Norte* (alone
up north).

Alone in my misery, I decided to ease the frightful
thought of being a one-man picking machine by calling
upon a few of my friends to form a bachelor picking crew.
Each of us had different reasons for wanting to join. Most
of us wanted an opportunity to make money. Some
wanted an opportunity to prove something, while the rest
had no choice. Six bachelors coming together to form
another harvesting machine, a crew to be viewed from a
safe distance, faceless bodies with nameless identities, less
noticeable than an idle brand-name tractor.

An extended family was born out of great necessity.
José, my brother, was the oldest of the group. He
provided us with historical data necessary for trivia bets
made on old song titles or old rock-and-roll bands.
Miguel was the cool *vato* of the group, possessing a Fonz-
like attitude that would enable him to serve as our
ambassador for our upcoming summer relationships. We
all felt that his great sex appeal derived from his curly

Samson-type hair, a theory that was put to rest after our perms failed to attract anything but ridiculing looks. Jaime was a beer-guzzling, Village People lover who seemed to believe that cruising with Spanish radio commercials was a display of cutting-edge cruising. Alfonso was a sixteen-year-old delinquent looking at our trip north as an alternative to juvenile hall. Then there was Mario, a soft-spoken twenty-year-old, owning Hollywood looks that complemented his good heart and his killer smile. Mario's reason for joining the group was made clear to all of us, announcing his twenty-first birthday *pachanga* in the fall. The remainder of his earnings would be invested in his lowrider.

Our journey north was made in three cars, a journey that provided us with our first cool ride to *el Norte*. Each car consisted of a driver and a shotgun copilot. Drivers were exchanged at every rest stop or pit stop for a much faster and safer trip. On our way, we enjoyed fast food instead of sandwiches, unlike in previous years, and we had a chance to sleep without anybody's stinky feet on our faces.

Our first destination was McMinnville, Oregon, a makeshift labor camp of a half-dozen trailers that were owned by Mr. Smith. We lived in a single trailer that had two bedrooms, one small bath, an even smaller kitchen, and a horrible living room. Upon arriving a meeting was called to pick roommates and to discuss living conditions. Rules were discussed and voted on, rules that were absolutely necessary for our survival as bachelors. Each team would take turns cooking, cleaning, and grocery shopping. There would be no smoking, no drinking, and no pissing on the toilet seat cover. We all agreed on the rules, carrying with us unspoken intentions of breaking every single one of them.

Our first day at work was just like any other first day of previous years. It was cold and wet, but the idea of working for ourselves got us started, cheered on by the songs that blasted out of the plastic box on top of our ancient wheelbarrows. Lunchtime, however, made us yearn for our mothers' warm *tacos*. As we opened our soggy Wonder-bread sandwiches that flopped back and forth, they spat out the jalapeños and purple onions to the ground. Instead of complaining, we remembered what we had been taught in past years: our circumstance was not for pleasure but for money. We were trying to get into a state of mind that would set our goals straight in times of great weakness.

Our first bachelor dinner was prepared by Team A, chefs José and Jaime. Their specialty consisted of *papas*, *chorizo,* and eggs and of course some refried, refried canned beans. After dinner we all took naps followed by a relaxing game of poker that ended up in a senseless argument, forcing teammates to swap partners due to irreconcilable differences. For breakfast we all had Hostess preservatives and instant coffee sweetened with countless eye-opening scoops of sugar.

Our determination to be the best in the field was fierce as we worked past all the other *familias*. We did have a little trouble with the rookies on our team, taking the time to show them our trade secrets, which didn't seem to help much. Once in a while we teased each other about midnight explosions that no one would claim. Matchups with the local *gueritas* (white girls) were also fun, especially if one of the guys hated his chosen partner. I guess our first week went as good as could be expected for six bachelors.

Eventually, most if not all of the rules were broken. After a week of variations with potatoes, eggs, and beans in combination with our increasing frustrations, a call was made for a change of plans. The new changes forced everyone to be responsible for his own dinner, his own cleanliness, and his own beer. Instead of improving things, our new rules gave way to anarchy as cleanliness became extinct and our frustration again called for another overhaul. By this time our internal problems were known around the camp, creating a nickname for our rebellious group. We became known as *"Los Sebos,"* a residue of lard-type origin.

To everyone's surprise, most of our domestic problems were resolved except for the lingering problem of second-hand smoke. I was outnumbered concerning this nasty habit, as even democracy failed to help me. I decided to overrule their vote by sabotaging their self-destructive habit. I planned a covert operation that called for the creation of volatile cigarettes with varied timed explosions. This was done by selecting several cigarettes from each pack and removing half of the tobacco from each. Then several match heads were inserted into the cigarette and repacked with the extracted tobacco. The explosive cigarettes were then randomly inserted back into each pack, making the loaded cigarettes indistinguishable even to my knowing eyes.

Alfonso was the first victim. The explosion nearly burned his eyelashes and eyebrow on the right side of his face. Other explosions followed, creating great fear among the chain-smokers. Some of them starting talk about a possible lawsuit, and others felt that *brujeria* (witchcraft) was involved. Changing cigarette brands was their next alternative, but it only gave them the same results with bigger explosions. The smoked-filled room became bearable since my revenge provided me with entertainment for the evenings. However, when Jaime's shirt caught on fire I was forced to stop my scheme, and I hesitantly revealed my evil deeds but threatened to continue if their indoor smoking persisted. My subversive act had worked, granting me the power to overrule their democratic advantage. Mysteriously, cigarette consumption dropped significantly from then on, and only alcohol consumption could remove their suspicious inhibitions.

It had been a weak strawberry season, making it harder to achieve our daily monetary goals. With the bad crop came the perfect reason to stay home, first José, then Mario, alternating days to be less suspicious. José's reasons were obviously psychological, as opposed to Mario's, which were purely physical. Mario complained of dizziness and stomach cramps that seemed normal to us, especially after the demanding labor. Mr. Smith, our *patrón* (boss), had announced his intentions of picking the strawberry fields three more times in order to meet his required crop quota. Failure to meet this quota would mean less profit since he would be fined for not meeting his projected minimum crop tonnage. For us, the failure to move on and not meet our daily goals would mean a loss of morale, profit, and time. We figured that even without our presence Mr. Smith would still have enough pickers to meet his demand. So we decided to take a gamble and bail out, each one of us giving Mr. Smith his personal reason for our quick departure. Our announcement was not well received, eliminating any future possibilities of work at this farm or any other nearby.

Our new destination gave us high hopes, as Miguel inquired about the strawberry season in Washington State. Sakuma Farms was said to be starting soon and expected the best strawberry crop in years. Up to this point every decision that we had made had been considered ignorant by critical eyes. All that had changed since our strategic move, putting us in the driver's seat and marking the way for all the rest to continue north.

Sakuma Farms was one of the biggest employers of summer field labor in the entire state of Washington. Its actual numbers had risen steadily throughout the years, giving them several thousand workers in a good year. They were housed at three separate labor camps located a few miles just outside of town. All three camps were inhabited by migrant workers that traveled from as far south as Mexico and Texas, and as far east as Michigan. There was a fourth labor camp, strictly inhabited by Native Americans, segregated for reasons that I never understood.

Our party of six was assigned to a labor camp that was located next to a mountain known to be inhabited by temperamental cattle, summer lovers, and someone who couldn't quite make it to one of the camp's communal bathrooms. We were given two keys for two cabins, rooms that had been occupied by Miguel's family the previous twelve years. The group was split into two. Miguel, José, and I shared one cabin, while Jaime, Mario, and Alfonso occupied another. Our cabins weren't much to look at since the structure itself desperately needed a paint job and a couple of the windows were cracked. Each structure was divided into four rooms by quarter-inch plywood decorated with ghostly names, love hearts, and man-made holes filled with colorful gum and toilet paper. A gas stove, a small sink, a fifties refrigerator, two double-sized bunk beds, and a Playschool dinner table decorated our new living quarters. A piece of tin acted as a roof, a noisemaker that exaggerated the slightest drizzle into torrential rain. The cabin's greatest asset was its location, giving us closer access to one of the two communal bathrooms, and providing us with a view of at least 50 percent of the camp's single *chicas*. Also, a rather large, open field served as a makeshift playing area. Although not quite a five-star accommodation, it was a place to live. Our timely arrival on a Saturday gave us an extra day to unpack, clean up, and rest a little before we awoke to another harvest run.

The strawberry harvest was the best any of us had picked in years. The enthusiasm of possibly reaching our financial goals made us work even harder, leaving us completely exhausted at the end of each day. There were times when even making dinner was waived for a few more hours of rest. By the end of the first week, José and Mario began taking days off again. For days we came home to find José bathing in Vicks VapoRub, saying that his allergies and his lingering summer cold were driving him crazy. We kept wondering if the chics dug the smell of Vicks, a thought that came to mind every time we found José sharing fumes with his latest squeeze. Mario, on the other hand, was less of a showman, only saying that he didn't feel good and that he was going to take it easy for a few days. Alfonso eventually joined in, flipping us off whenever the alarm went off.

We finished the strawberry season in mid-July giving us better-than-expected earnings. As we entered the raspberry season, most of the group were already calling the summer a great success. Right when things started to look great, though, the raspberry season began to decline. An overabundance of pickers forced quicker picking passes of the raspberry fields, producing fewer and fewer quantities of fruit.

In turn our picking days became shorter. We sometimes found ourselves back at the camp by 10:30 a.m. The shorter days only encouraged José, Alfonso, and Mario to continue staying home. We had counted on the raspberry season to provide us with more money. Instead, we found ourselves using our savings, spending more on our appetites than what we earned. Suddenly things began to turn on us. Everything began to look and feel differently. Families began searching for work elsewhere, forcing many of them to move on.

My parents had followed our cue when we left Oregon by following us to Washington State. They lived on the opposite end of the camp, which rarely gave me the opportunity to see them except for periodic meetings in the fields. During one of these encounters my *jefa* had mentioned to me that my sister Vita and her husband would be arriving any day. My mother had requested my sister's help in changing my father's mind about sticking around for the rest of the summer. Apparently my father had been suffering from serious health problems. My sister's job was to convince him to return home to receive affordable medical attention in Mexicali. Work was something that he had never walked away from, even under questionable health conditions. However, the presence of his favorite daughter and the disappointing raspberry crop softened his ego.

During this time Mario began looking a bit weak. His small frame appeared tired and frail, and his working days had been sporadic since our arrival in Washington. Sometimes he only worked one day out of the week. We knew that he had fallen in love with a girl from Yakima, who had left during the exodus of the bad raspberry season. The intensity of his love was obvious by the lengthy letters he wrote everyday. Since he didn't seem to be in any physical pain, we diagnosed him with a severe case of chronic *lovenosis*.

My parents were scheduled to leave at noon on a Friday. Leaving with them would be the Benedict Arnolds, José and Alfonso, who were cowering from the remaining raspberry season and the backbreaking cucumber harvest. I left work that day at 11:00 a.m., making sure that I had plenty of time to say good-bye to my parents. Just as I expected, my parents were leaving with mixed feelings. On one hand, my father would receive the medical attention he was willing to pay for. On the other hand, the scorching desert heat would welcome them home, keeping them prisoners for the remainder of the summer. Looking into the brown van, I could barely see through their packed belongings: two pet-store rabbits in a cage, fishing rods, second-hand clothes, and multicolored blankets. As I took a closer look inside, I was able to spot José and Alfonso in the back seat waiting anxiously, waving at me with a hasty good-bye. Somehow I knew they would suffer for their abandonment of our group, knowing that the rabbit crap and urine would be difficult to endure during the trip back home.

As my parents drove away, I stood there and watched them disappear behind the obtrusive mountain landscape.

Their departure left me with an irrepressible feeling of pride. I had outlasted them, an accomplishment worthy of respect. My parents' departure also left me with a variety of groceries: a bag of sugar, a loaf of bread, salsa, hot jalapeños, Twinkies, ice cream, and a dozen or so day-old tortillas. Flowers that would have been confiscated at the Oregon-California border were donated to me, a gift that would be passed on to the girl of my choice.

I had agreed to meet Miguel and Jaime back at the raspberry field at 1:00 p.m., which gave me enough time to eat something at our cabin. We were going to be off work the next several days, so we decided to go on a job hunt at the surrounding berry farms. As I unpacked the groceries, I stopped next door and peeked into Mario's room to say "hi." I found him in deep thought, writing another letter to his summer love. He acknowledged me after I broke his concentration with a teasing remark. I asked him how he was feeling, a question that had been asked a lot lately. Smiling, he answered me in a soft, scratchy voice, "I'm okay." It was a reply that had become too familiar.

I hurried back to use our donated salsa and tortillas to prepare a satisfying meal around my greasy *torta de huevo* (egg omelet). I abandoned my quick lunch after noticing that my time was almost up. After locking my cabin, I remembered the flowers I had left on the top of the car.

Cursing at myself, I ran to the car and grabbed them.
Then I ran back to Mario's cabin so I could ask him if he
would flower-sit until I returned later that afternoon. He
didn't seem to mind my intrusion, and he continued to
write his lengthy letter. Out of courtesy I asked him if he
was interested in going out to look for work that
afternoon, but he responded with a "no," saying that he
wanted to finish some important things. "I'll probably go
with you guys tomorrow instead," he said in a joking
manner, knowing very well he would not be joining us. I
laid the flowers on the miniature dining table and walked
out, telling him I would see him later.

Picking at the Sakuma raspberry fields ended around
2:00 p.m., which gave us enough time to search for jobs
on the surrounding farms. Luck was on our side that day
as our second stop found us work, which provided us with
a reason to celebrate. We arrived back at the camp at
3:45 p.m., looking forward to a long shower and a cold
beer. I was still trying to decide who would be the lucky
recipient of the flowers, eventually deciding that Leticia
would be the girl. We expected Mario to be in his usual
afternoon location, standing by the front door looking out
while waiting for the camp's girls to strut their stuff as
they headed to the bathroom. Instead, we found both
doors closed. Miguel and I unlocked our cabin while
Jaime remained outside knocking on Mario's door,

waiting for him to open up. We became concerned after Mario failed to respond to the racket we made. Since the door was unlocked, all we had to do was pick the inside latch. With a butter knife in hand, I struggled to unfasten it. A moment later I opened it by tapping the latch as Jaime pulled the door.

Miguel was the first to go in, followed by Jaime. Jaime looked for Mario on one of the top bunk beds. We expected him to be in deep sleep. Instead we found him folded backwards on the ground. Miguel picked him up, thinking that he must have fallen off the bed and had passed out. The dry blood smeared on the side of his mouth was not a good sign. We refused to believe the worst possible truth. No! He couldn't be! "Let's feel his pulse!" I shouted. I reached over to grab his wrist while Miguel and Jaime suspended his frail body in their arms. Grabbing his arm, I felt the coldness of his skin and the stiffness of his joints. His pulse was missing. We refused to recognize the lifeless body as Mario's. He was full of life, full of joy. He had plans. Mario was going to celebrate his life with us and we were all going to pitch in for his upcoming birthday *pachanga*.

We continued in our disbelief, refusing to accept this was happening. It couldn't be true. Conflicting thoughts raced through our minds, one after another, thoughts echoed by the pounding of our hearts. Death lay just a few feet away, revealing to us our own insignificance, our own mortality, and the unpredictablity of our lives. If we had a future it would be a hodgepodge of *ganas*, luck, faith, curiosity, love, and good friends.

Ultimately, a vicious anger set in and left us with no alternative but to curse at anything and anyone we felt was responsible for Mario's death. We realized that we weren't in control of our lives, that we never would be. We had come this far looking for a way to better our lives. Instead, we had gained an endless supply of unanswered questions. Why did he die? Why not someone else? Why should we even continue with our lives?

Mario would never be forgotten. He would remain a good friend who had accompanied us through one of the most difficult period of our lives. We came to the realization that the time we had spent with Mario was insufficient. Just like the money we earned that summer.